LOVE YOURSELF

LAURASIA MATTINGLY

LOVE Yourself

100 EMPOWERING AFFIRMATIONS
TO CELEBRATE YOU

Hand Lettering by Alyssa González

ROCKRIDGE
PRESS

Interior and Cover Designer: Carlos Esparza
Art Producer: Janice Ackerman
Editor: Crystal Nero
Production Editor: Jenna Dutton

Hand Lettering: ©2021 Alyssa González
Author photo courtesy of Madison Chertow

ISBN: Print   978-1-64876-677-0
       eBook 978-1-64876-174-4
R0

For my mother, Lourdes, my constant teacher in life and now in spirit. For my father, Jack, my own living Buddha.

To all beings, everywhere, who are learning to love themselves a little more each day.

✳ INTRODUCTION

I'm Laurasia Mattingly, a meditation and mindfulness teacher. I'm here
to share with you the magic and transformation that affirmations can
have on your life. Self-love is a lifelong journey, but ultimately one I
believe everyone should be on. My personal journey with self-love has
been a treacherous one, but once I began intentionally practicing more
self-love, my quality of life started to improve tremendously.

My mother passed away when I was 20 years old. My self-worth was
low, and I sought validation from people, places, and things outside of
myself. Through meditation—and, more specifically, affirmations—I
learned that one cannot love unless they love themself first. I learned
true healing comes from the acceptance of who we are, and learning to
love it all. I learned, and still continue to learn, to love all parts of myself,
on the good days, the bad days, and everything in between. And I've
come to learn that the moment we choose ourselves, the world chooses
us back.

My intention with this book is to inspire you to get started on your
self-love journey, or perhaps help you deepen a self-love practice you
may already have. Affirmations can be used as a little self-love boost at
any time of day, whether you prefer to use them when you wake up to

set the tone for your day, in the middle of the day when you need a little reminder, or as the last thing before you go to sleep. As you incorporate them into your life, you'll find that affirmations celebrate the unique magic that is you!

This book can be read chronologically, but does not have to be. You can flip to any page, at any time, to get some inspiration for your day. You can go back and forth, or navigate the book in the way that feels most organic to you. It's here as your little self-love guidebook to use when you are looking for some support in areas like love, work, or difficult emotions. You'll find it filled with little nuggets that will guide you, inspire you, and ultimately bring you back to your true nature: love.

And it all begins with loving yourself.

IN COMMITTING TO MY HEALING, I COMMIT TO SELF-LOVE.

AS I MARVEL AT THE
MIRACLE THAT IS ME,
TODAY I TAKE A MOMENT TO
APPRECIATE THE WONDER
OF THE HUMAN HEART.
I THANK THE BEATS THAT
CARRY ON, DAY AND NIGHT,
EVEN WHILE I'M UNAWARE.

THERE IS NO "RIGHT"
OR "WRONG" WAY
TO FEEL. IN THIS
MOMENT, I EMBRACE
WHAT IT FEELS LIKE
TO BE ME.

I ASK FOR WHAT I WANT BECAUSE I AM WORTHY AND DESERVING OF HAVING IT. I HONOR MY DESIRES AND NEEDS FULLY TODAY.

I WILL GIVE MY INNER CRITIC THE DAY OFF TODAY. ITS OPINIONS AND JUDGMENTS WILL NOT HOLD POWER OVER ME.

MY BODY IS A VESSEL
THAT ALLOWS ME
TO EXPERIENCE THE
PHYSICAL WORLD.
TODAY I CHOOSE TO
HONOR AND BE AT
PEACE WITH MY BODY.

FEELING DEEPLY IS
A SIGN I AM AWAKE,
EXPERIENCING THE
FULL TEXTURE OF LIFE.
DEPTH OF EMOTION
IS PART OF BEING
WONDERFULLY HUMAN.

I KNOW THAT
MISSTEPS ALONG
THE PATH ARE ALSO
TEACHING ME. TWO
STEPS FORWARD
AND ONE STEP BACK
IS STILL A STEP
FORWARD.

TODAY I VISIT THE PAST AND FUTURE GENTLY, KNOWING THAT RUMINATION AND ANXIETY ARE NATURAL TENDENCIES OF THE MIND. I WELCOME GROUNDING THOUGHTS, NOT WHAT-IFS.

MY BODY IS MINE AND MINE ALONE. I WILL TREAT IT WITH THE RESPECT IT DESERVES TODAY.

PAIN IS NOT WRONG.
REACTING TO PAIN AS WRONG INITIATES
THE TRANCE OF UNWORTHINESS.
THE MOMENT WE BELIEVE
SOMETHING IS WRONG, OUR WORLD
SHRINKS AND WE LOSE OURSELVES
IN THE EFFORT TO COMBAT
OUR PAIN.

Tara Brach
PSYCHOLOGIST + AUTHOR

I AM WORTHY OF BEING SEEN
AND HEARD, EVEN IF PEOPLE
WON'T ALWAYS AGREE WITH
MY THOUGHTS AND ACTIONS.
SOMETIMES I WILL MAKE
MISTAKES, SOMETIMES I WILL
BE WRONG. AT LEAST I KNOW
I'M BEING REAL.

I REALIZE THAT EVERY SINGLE BEING EXPERIENCES DIFFICULTIES; WHEN I SUFFER, I AM NOT ALONE. RATHER THAN BEING HARD ON MYSELF IN THESE DIFFICULT MOMENTS, I WILL BE KIND.

MY MIND IS LIKE A
GARDEN, WITH SEEDS
FOR JOY AND SEEDS
FOR SUFFERING.
THE SEEDS I WATER
ARE THE SEEDS
THAT GROW.

I AM GRATEFUL FOR
WHAT MY BODY
ALLOWS ME TO DO
EACH DAY, EVEN IF
THAT SIMPLY MEANS
SITTING MINDFULLY IN
STILLNESS.

HOW I FEEL IN THIS MOMENT IS COMPLETELY VALID. IT'S OKAY TO NOT ALWAYS FEEL "OKAY."

I WAS PUT HERE ON THIS EARTH TO BE MY MOST AUTHENTIC SELF. I KNOW THAT THIS LOOKS DIFFERENT FOR EVERYONE. NO TWO PATHS ARE THE SAME. MY PATH IS MY OWN, AND TODAY, I EMBRACE IT.

IT'S OKAY TO NOT
HAVE ALL THE
ANSWERS YET, OR
HAVE EVERYTHING
FIGURED OUT.
LET MY MIND BE
CURIOUS INSTEAD OF
CONTROLLING.

NO ONE'S BODY
IS "PERFECT."
I RECOGNIZE THE
BEAUTY OF MY
UNIQUE PHYSICAL
SELF, AND LOVE
IT AS IT IS TODAY.

SOMETIMES WE HAVE
TO DO THINGS WE
ARE AFRAID OF. TODAY,
INSTEAD OF RUNNING
FROM A FEAR, I WILL
EXAMINE WHY IT SCARES
ME, AND MOVE FORWARD.

TODAY, I WILL TRY
NOT TO ASSIGN JUDGMENT
TO THINGS, PEOPLE, OR
EXPERIENCES BY LOOKING AT
THEM AS "GOOD" OR "BAD,"
"RIGHT" OR "WRONG." I WILL
EXPERIENCE THE FREEDOM OF
A LIFE WITHOUT LABELS.

I DON'T NEED TO RELY ON THE EXTERNAL VALIDATION OF OTHERS. I WILL RELY ON MY OWN HEART TO REAFFIRM MY GREATNESS.

I APPRECIATE MY BODY FOR GETTING ME UP EVERY DAY; IT BRINGS ME ONE DAY CLOSER TO ACHIEVING MY DREAMS.

I REALIZE THAT MY THOUGHTS ARE REAL, BUT NOT NECESSARILY THE TRUTH. TODAY I WILL MEET MY THOUGHTS WITH DISCERNMENT BEFORE I DEFINE THEM.

WHEN I ALLOW MYSELF THE FREEDOM TO FULLY FEEL MY FEELINGS, I UNBLOCK THE PATHWAY TO HEALING.

WHEN STRESS ARISES,
I WILL SEE IT AS
A SIGN TO LET GO OF
MY NEED TO CONTROL.
I WILL FIND SOME
COMFORT IN
THE DISCOMFORT
OF THE UNKNOWN.

I ACCEPT MYSELF AS I AM TODAY, WHATEVER THAT LOOKS LIKE AND HOWEVER THAT FEELS.

TODAY I WILL HONOR MY ANGER AND RECOGNIZE IT AS A NATURAL REACTION TO NOT FULLY UNDERSTANDING. I WILL BE OPEN TO THAT WHICH I DO NOT FULLY KNOW.

TODAY I WILL SUPPORT THE LIFE I WISH TO CREATE.

RATHER THAN LIVE
WITH THE REGRET OF
NOT SPEAKING UP,
I WILL RISK SAYING
WHAT IS ON MY
MIND TODAY.

TODAY, MY INNER BEAUTY WILL HONOR MY OUTER BEAUTY. MY BODY IS UNIQUE IN COLOR, SHAPE, AND SIZE; THAT IS WHAT MAKES ME SO AMAZING.

As surely as there is a

VOYAGE

away, there is a

JOURNEY

home.

JACK KORNFIELD AUTHOR

I DON'T NEED TO FEEL GUILTY FOR REMOVING TOXIC PEOPLE FROM MY LIFE.

I TRUST THAT
EVERYTHING IN LIFE—
THE GOOD, THE BAD,
AND THE THINGS
IN BETWEEN—IS
TEACHING ME AND
HELPING ME GROW.

MY MIND CAN WANDER
OFF INTO FEARS
OF THE FUTURE OR
MEMORIES OF THE
PAST, BUT I ALWAYS
HAVE THE ABILITY TO
RETURN HOME TO THE
PRESENT MOMENT.

MY EXHAUSTION IS
A SIGN THAT IT IS
TIME TO SLOW DOWN.
TODAY I WILL VIEW
MY EXHAUSTION AS
SACRED, AND I WILL
ALLOW MYSELF SOME
RESTORATIVE REST.

IT'S OKAY TO FEEL
SAD. I KNOW THAT
WHEN THE HEART
BREAKS, IT'S NOT
BREAKING DOWN—IT'S
BREAKING OPEN TO
NEW LIFE.

I AM INSPIRED BY MY OWN JOURNEY, BECAUSE I KNOW THAT EVERY STEP I TAKE IS LEADING ME WHERE I NEED TO GO.

WHEN I AM COMPASSIONATE
TOWARD MY OWN THOUGHTS,
I'M ABLE TO BE MORE
COMPASSIONATE TOWARD OTHER
PEOPLE AND THEIR OPINIONS.
I UNDERSTAND EVERYONE
HAS A RIGHT TO THEIR OWN
PERSPECTIVE, NO MATTER HOW
DIFFERENT IT MAY BE FROM MINE.

ALTHOUGH MY BODY
MAY HOLD ON TO
TRAUMA FROM THE
PAST, IT HAS THE
AMAZING ABILITY TO
UNLEARN AND WRITE
A NEW STORY.

ANGER, SADNESS, FRUSTRATION, AND BEING OVERWHELMED ALL AFFIRM MY ALIVENESS. THEY'RE PROVING TO ME THAT IT IS BETTER TO FEEL DEEPLY THAN TO NOT FEEL AT ALL.

I CELEBRATE THE MIRACLE OF MY ALIVENESS. I CELEBRATE THE GIFT OF ANOTHER DAY. I CHERISH THIS CHANCE TO BE A PART OF THIS EARTH, TO BREATHE THIS AIR, AND TO ENJOY THE SYMPHONY OF THE SOUNDS OF THE WORLD.

he who is not
every day conquering
some fear has not
learned the secret
of life.

RALPH WALDO EMERSON

I WELCOME IN CHANGE WITH OPEN ARMS. CHANGE MIGHT NOT ALWAYS BE EASY, BUT IT IS NECESSARY FOR MY GROWTH. WHAT NEW POSSIBILITIES ARE OUT THERE WAITING?

I AM BECOMING AWARE OF
MY HABITUAL THOUGHTS.
SINCE MY THOUGHTS CREATE
MY WORLD, I AM ABLE TO
CREATE JOY IN MY LIFE
WHEN I FOCUS ON JOYOUS
THOUGHTS.

I LISTEN TO MY
BODY AND TEND TO
ITS NEEDS WITH
COMPASSION AND
KINDNESS.

I AM OPEN AND ACCEPTING TO THE FACT THAT LIFE CAN BE AN EMOTIONAL ROLLER COASTER. THE UPS AND DOWNS ARE A PART OF THIS BEAUTIFUL JOURNEY.

IN THE CHAOS OF THINGS, TODAY I REMEMBER THAT EVERY MOMENT IS SHAPING WHO I AM AND WHO I AM MEANT TO BE.

THOUGHTS THAT ARISE WITHIN
ME DO NOT DETERMINE WHO
I AM. AN ANXIOUS THOUGHT
DOES NOT MEAN I'M AN ANXIOUS
PERSON. AN ANGRY THOUGHT
DOES NOT MEAN I'M AN ANGRY
PERSON. EVERY HUMAN HAS
THE CAPACITY FOR ALL
TYPES OF THOUGHTS.

MY BODY IS SACRED.
I WILL TREAT MY
BODY TODAY AS I
WOULD MY BEST
FRIEND: WITH TENDER
THOUGHTS AND
HONEST CARE.

CHALLENGING MY OWN LONG-HELD THOUGHTS OFFERS OPPORTUNITY TO TRANSFORM MY PERSPECTIVE AND SEE SITUATIONS WITH NEW UNDERSTANDING.

IT'S OKAY TO FEEL
LOST. TODAY I WILL
TURN MY FEAR
OF BEING LOST
INTO WONDER AND
CURIOSITY.

STRESS IS A NORMAL HUMAN EMOTION. I WILL GIVE MYSELF WHATEVER ADDITIONAL SUPPORT I NEED TODAY, WHETHER IT'S MEDITATION, SURROUNDING MYSELF WITH NATURE, OR WHATEVER HEALTHY ACTION I NEED TO EASE MY NERVES.

Remember,
you have been criticizing
yourself for years
and it hasn't worked.
Try approving of yourself
and see what happens.

LOUISE HAY AUTHOR, MOTIVATIONAL SPEAKER

TODAY I WILL NOT COMPARE MYSELF TO OTHER PEOPLE'S PHYSICAL FITNESS. I UNDERSTAND THERE IS NO "SECRET" TO GOOD HEALTH OTHER THAN A PERSONALIZED EXERCISE, NUTRITION, AND HEALING PLAN. TODAY I WILL MEET ANY FEELINGS OF UNWORTHINESS WITH COMPASSION, AND I WILL TAKE WISE ACTION.

WHEN I TAKE A MOMENT
TO BREATHE, I FIND
PEACE AMID SUFFERING.
MY BREATH SOFTENS
WHATEVER IS ARISING
IN THIS MOMENT, AND
I KNOW I AM OKAY.

JUST LIKE SPRING
DOES NOT RUSH
TO SUMMER, I AM
RIGHT ON TIME.
THERE IS NO NEED
TO RUSH MY LIFE.

DESPITE WHAT IT MIGHT LOOK LIKE ON THE OUTSIDE, NO ONE HAS LIFE FIGURED OUT. WHEN I FEEL OVERWHELMED, I REMIND MYSELF THAT I'M DOING THE BEST I CAN.

HOWEVER SICK, HOWEVER
HEALTHY, HOWEVER AGED,
HOWEVER YOUNG, HOWEVER
WEAK, HOWEVER STRONG,
I CELEBRATE MY BODY AS
IT IS TODAY.

IF I FEEL UNWORTHY,
I REMIND MYSELF THAT
I AM ENOUGH, I AM
CAPABLE, AND I AM
DESERVING OF LOVE.

SUCCESS IS MINE
WHEN I FOLLOW WHAT
FEELS RIGHT. ANYTHING
NOT IN ALIGNMENT WITH
MY HIGHEST GOOD IS
A SIGN THAT IT'S TIME
TO LET GO.

TODAY I WILL TAKE A MOMENT TO ENJOY LIFE'S SIMPLE PLEASURES AND PUT MY MIND AT EASE. THE PAST IS GONE, AND THE FUTURE IS NOT YET HERE. I WILL SAVOR THE LITTLE JOYS OF NOW, LIKE THE SUN WARMING MY FACE, THE SOUND OF THE WIND, THE SMELL OF FRESH-CUT GRASS.

MY PHYSICAL BODY
RESPONDS TO MY
SUBCONSCIOUS
BELIEFS. TODAY I WILL
BE MINDFUL OF MY
THOUGHTS, KNOWING
THEY WILL MANIFEST IN
MY PHYSICAL FORM.

BY ESTABLISHING HEALTHY
BOUNDARIES WITH OTHERS,
I HONOR MY WELL-BEING.
ACTS OF SELF-PRESERVATION
ALLOW ME TO SHOW
UP IN THE WORLD AS
MY BEST SELF.

STOP THINKING YOUR WAY THROUGH LIFE, ALWAYS TRYING TO WORK IT OUT BEFORE LIVING IT. LIFE IS TO BE LIVED, NOT ANALYZED TO DEATH. FEEL.

JEFF FOSTER AUTHOR

EVERY PAST
RELATIONSHIP HAS
TAUGHT ME WHAT I
DESIRE, AND DO NOT
DESIRE, IN A PARTNER.
BOTH ARE VALUABLE
LESSONS.

FRUSTRATION IS A
PLACE OF UNANSWERED
QUESTIONS AND
PROBLEMS NOT YET
SOLVED, AND I WILL
NOT FEAR IT.

I TRUST THAT MY
INTENTIONS WILL
MANIFEST IF THEY
ARE IN ALIGNMENT
WITH MY HIGHEST
GOOD.

INTIMACY ISN'T ALWAYS EASY.
LEARNING TO LOVE MY BODY
FULLY IS A LIFELONG JOURNEY;
SHARING MY BODY WITH
ANOTHER PERSON IS ANOTHER
LIFELONG JOURNEY. I AM OPEN
TO LEARNING ABOUT MY OWN,
ANOTHER'S, AND OUR
MUTUAL PLEASURE.

TODAY I WILL MEASURE
MY SUCCESS BY HOW
MANY TIMES I SMILE.
BONUS POINTS IF I MAKE
ANOTHER PERSON SMILE.

I AM MORE THAN MY
JOB TITLE AND MY
ACCOMPLISHMENTS.
I REACH FAR BEYOND
WHAT SOCIETY THINKS
IS VALUABLE. I AM ME.
AND I AM WORTHY.

I AM AWARE OF HOW MY
EMOTIONS CONNECT TO
AND AFFECT MY BODY.
TODAY I WILL MOVE
MY BODY, IN ANY WAY
POSSIBLE, TO GET
THOSE EMOTIONS
MOVING AND FLOWING.

SOMETIMES LIFE FEELS SO SERIOUS. TODAY I WILL INVITE MORE LIGHTHEARTEDNESS AND PLAYFULNESS.

I REALIZE I CAN HAVE MY OWN OPINIONS WITHOUT JUDGING THE UNIQUENESS OF OTHER PEOPLE. TODAY I WILL MEET OTHERS WITH AN OPEN MIND, AND WELCOME NEW PERSPECTIVES.

SOMETIMES MY BODY
CHALLENGES ME. TODAY I
WILL SEE THESE CHALLENGES
AS A SIGN TO LISTEN TO MY
BODY, RATHER THAN ALWAYS
TELLING IT WHAT TO DO.

I AM RESILIENT. I HAVE THE ABILITY TO GET BACK UP WHEN LIFE KNOCKS ME DOWN. I HAVE THE ABILITY TO CRACK A SMILE AFTER A GOOD CRY. I HAVE THE ABILITY TO HEAL AFTER HEARTBREAK. I HAVE THE ABILITY TO FORGIVE AFTER I GET ANGRY. NO EMOTIONAL SETBACK IS PERMANENT.

WE CAN FREE
OURSELVES FROM THE
OLD STORIES THAT HAVE
REDUCED US AND ALLOW
REAL LOVE FOR OURSELVES
TO BLOSSOM.

SHARON SALZBERG
AUTHOR

TO BRING PEACE
TO MY LIFE, I MUST
BE MINDFUL OF MY
THOUGHTS. TODAY
I WILL WEED OUT
NEGATIVITY AND
FOCUS ON SELF-
LOVING THOUGHTS.

I UNDERSTAND MY
BODY IS FUNCTIONING
AS BEST AS IT CAN
IN THIS MOMENT. FOR
THAT, I AM THANKFUL.

RESENTMENT CAN FESTER INSIDE OF ME AND CAUSE SUFFERING. I WILL ACCEPT THAT FORGIVENESS ISN'T SAYING THAT BAD BEHAVIOR IS OKAY, BUT IS LETTING GO OF WHATEVER IS STOPPING ME FROM FINDING PEACE.

WHEN I OVERCOMPLICATE
A SITUATION, I WILL TAKE
A STEP BACK TO NARROW
MY FOCUS SO I CAN BETTER
UNDERSTAND WHAT IS
GOING ON. I WILL RECOGNIZE
THAT FINDING EASE
MIGHT TAKE TIME.

I WILL CARRY MY BODY IN A WAY THAT PROUDLY SHOWS MY INNER BEAUTY AND STRENGTH.

DIFFICULT EMOTIONS ARE NOT AN ILLNESS, BUT RATHER A SIGNAL OF WHERE I CAN MEET MYSELF WITH MORE TENDERNESS AND HEALING.

ANXIETY DOESN'T TELL ME
THE TRUTH; IT AWAKENS
THE STORIES I TELL MYSELF.
TODAY I WILL BREATHE
INTO THE MOMENT, EASING
INTO WHAT I KNOW TO BE
ACTUALLY TRUE.

I HONOR MY BODY AND SET IT UP FOR SUCCESS BY LEARNING WHAT WORKS BEST. HOW MUCH SLEEP IT NEEDS, WHAT TYPE OF FOOD FEELS MOST NUTRITIOUS, AND WHAT TYPE OF MOVEMENT IT RESPONDS WELL TO ARE ALL EXCELLENT TOOLS IN GETTING TO KNOW MY BODY BETTER.

CHANGE CAN BE TOUGH AND
DISRUPTIVE EMOTIONALLY.
WHEN I HONOR MY FEELINGS
AND PRACTICE SELF-LOVE,
I CAN BEGIN TO SOFTEN
INTO THE CHANGE INSTEAD
OF MEETING IT WITH
HARSHNESS.

TODAY I INTEND TO LIVE LIFE, RATHER THAN THINK IT THROUGH. I WILL BE PRESENT TO EACH MOMENT THAT ARISES, RATHER THAN ANALYZING IT.

change
is the only
constant.
Heraclitus
greek philosopher

WHEN I FEEL I AM LACKING
IN MY PHYSICAL BODY,
I WILL CHECK IN WITH
MYSELF AND ASK: IS IT
SOMETHING I CAN WORK
TOWARD CHANGING? OR IS IT
A FEELING OF VALIDATION I
NEED TO CULTIVATE WITHIN?

LIFE CAN FEEL LIKE A BUMPY RIDE SOMETIMES. KINDNESS AND GENTLENESS TOWARD MYSELF AND OTHERS ACT LIKE SHOCK ABSORBERS, SMOOTHING OUT THE RIDE.

SOMETIMES IT'S HARD TO TELL THE DIFFERENCE BETWEEN URGENT AND IMPORTANT. TODAY I WILL TAKE A FEW DEEP BREATHS AND THINK BEFORE DECIDING ANY PLAN OF ACTION.

REST IS JUST AS IMPORTANT AS WORKING, BUT RARELY PRIORITIZED. TODAY I WILL HONOR THE NEED FOR RECHARGING, BEING KIND TO MYSELF WHEN I FIND I AM PUSHING TOO HARD.

GRIEF TENDS TO COME IN WAVES. LOSS OF A LOVED ONE, JOB, HOME, OR ANYTHING SPECIAL IS TOUGH. TODAY I WILL GIVE MYSELF THE SPACE TO MOURN.

I AM AWARE OF MY TALENTS, STRENGTHS, AND PASSIONS. WHEN I FIND MY MIND COMPARING MYSELF TO ANOTHER, I WILL PAUSE AND REMEMBER I AM MAGNIFICENT. WHEN THE GRASS LOOKS GREENER ON THE OTHER SIDE, I WILL REMEMBER TO WATER MY OWN LAWN WITH PRAISE AND SELF-LOVE.

I WILL NOT
UNDERESTIMATE
THE POWER OF A NAP
AND DEEP BREATHING.
THEY ARE OUR BODIES'
NATURAL TOOLS
FOR PEACE.

TRYING NEW THINGS CAN BE SCARY. BUT SOMETIMES BEING AFRAID IS GOOD, AS IT PUSHES ME OUT OF MY COMFORT ZONE, BRINGING ME PLACES I NEVER THOUGHT POSSIBLE.

I GIVE MYSELF PERMISSION TO DAYDREAM. DREAMS OF AN IDEAL FUTURE HELP ME GAIN CLARITY IN WHAT I TRULY DESIRE IN LIFE. FIGURING OUT WHERE I WANT TO GO IS THE ONLY WAY I CAN START PLANNING HOW TO GET THERE.

I AM AWAKENING TO MY SOUL'S HIGHEST PURPOSE. EVERY MOMENT IS LEADING ME TO WHERE I NEED TO BE.

go back and take care
of yourself. your body needs
you. your perceptions need you,
your feeling needs you.
the wounded child in you
needs you. your suffering
needs you to acknowledge it.

THICH NHAT HANH VIETNAMESE MONK

BEFORE BLAMING ANOTHER PERSON FOR AN ANNOYANCE, TODAY I WILL TAKE THE OPPORTUNITY TO INVESTIGATE WHAT INSIDE OF ME FINDS IT IRRITATING.

WHEN I REMAIN
CURIOUS, I LEAVE
SPACE IN MY MIND
FOR NEW IDEAS,
NEW POSSIBILITIES,
AND NEW STORIES
TO BE WRITTEN.

I CAN FEEL STRONG AND TIRED AT THE SAME TIME.

DOUBT CAN HINDER MY GROWTH. TODAY I WILL NOT UNDERESTIMATE MY OWN POWER AND PURPOSE.

SOMETIMES PHYSICAL PAIN
DOESN'T LEAVE MY BODY.
TODAY I WILL MEET IT WITH
KINDNESS, AND TRUST THAT
MY BODY KNOWS
WHAT TO DO.

I AM PERFECTLY IMPERFECT; MY UNIQUENESS IS A GIFT!

SOMETIMES I SEEK PHYSICAL
LOVE IN ANOTHER BEING
AND ANOTHER BODY. TODAY
I WILL ACCEPT THAT LOVE
STARTS WITHIN ME. I CAN
LOVE OTHERS ONLY WITH THE
OVERFLOW OF LOVE I HAVE
FOR MYSELF.

TOUGH ENDINGS CAN BE BEAUTIFUL NEW BEGINNINGS. TODAY I WILL TRUST WHAT ENTERS AND EXITS MY LIFE.

TODAY, I WILL NOT FEAR
GETTING OLDER, THE AGING
PROCESS, OR EVEN DEATH.
I WILL MEET THE CYCLE OF
THE BODY WITH TENDERNESS
AND GRACE, AND MAKE SURE
I AM FULLY LIVING.

THERE IS NOTHING WRONG WITH UNCERTAINTY. TODAY, I WILL ACCEPT THE UNFOLDING OF THE UNKNOWN.

The moment between what you once were, & who you are now becoming, is where the dance of life really takes place.

DR. BARBARA DE ANGELIS
AUTHOR & SELF HELP LEADER

✳ RESOURCES

Bstan-'dzin-rgya-mtsho, Dalai Lama XIV, and Desmond Tutu. *The Book of Joy: Lasting Happiness in a Changing World.* New York: Avery, 2016.

Delia, Lalah. *Vibrate Higher Daily: Live Your Power.* New York: HarperOne, 2019.

Kornfield, Jack. *A Path with Heart: A Guide Through the Perils and Promises of Spiritual Life.* New York: Bantam Books, 1993.

Mattingly, Laurasia. *Meditations on Self-Love: Daily Wisdom for Healing, Acceptance, and Joy.* Emeryville, CA: Rockridge Press, 2020.

Nhat Hanh, Thich. *No Mud, No Lotus: The Art of Transforming Suffering.* Berkeley, CA: Parallax Press, 2014.

✳ REFERENCES

Alexander, James. *Best Ralph Waldo Emerson Quotes*. Bath, UK: Crombie Jardine Publishing Limited, 2017.

Brach, Tara. *Radical Acceptance: Embracing Your Life with the Heart of a Buddha*. New York: Bantam, 2003.

Foster, Jeff. *The Way of Rest: Finding the Courage to Hold Everything in Love*. Boulder, CO: Sounds True, 2016.

GoodReads. "Barbara De Angelis Quotes." Accessed October 21, 2020. GoodReads.com/quotes/840611-the-moment-in-between-what-you -once-were-and-who.

Hay, Louise. *You Can Heal Your Life*. Carlsbad, CA: Hay House, 1984.

Kornfield, Jack. *After Ecstasy, the Laundry: How the Heart Grows Wise on the Spiritual Path*. New York: Bantam, 2000.

Kornfield, Jack. *No Time Like the Present: Finding Freedom, Love, and Joy Right Where You Are*. New York: Atria, 2018.

Mattingly, Laurasia. "Sit Society." Accessed October 27, 2020.
LaurasiaMattingly.com/sit-society.

Nhat Hanh, Thich. *Fear: Essential Wisdom for Getting Through the Storm*.
New York: HarperOne, 2012.

——. *Peace Is Every Step: The Path of Mindfulness in Everyday Life*.
New York: Bantam, 1991.

——. *Reconciliation: Healing the Inner Child*. Berkeley, CA:
Parallax Press, 2006.

Salzberg, Sharon. *Real Love: The Art of Mindful Connection*. London:
Bluebird, 2017.

Tiny Buddha. "Quotes by Heraclitus." Accessed March 8, 2020.
tinybuddha.com/wisdom-author/heraclitus.

ACKNOWLEDGMENTS

Thank you to all my meditation teachers and mentors who have guided me down this path of self-actualization. Thank you to my father, Jack, guiding me on this human plane, and to my angel mother, Lourdes, with her spiritual guidance from above. Thank you to all my healers who have helped me learn to love my "baggage," my trauma, and my wounds so much that they no longer hold me down, but instead help me rise above. Thank you, all my friends who have taught me that goodness and unconditional love exists. And thank you, Life, for teaching me to trust you, for allowing me to see the lessons in the difficulties, and reminding me that love exists in all—but that it first must begin with myself.

ABOUT THE AUTHOR

 **Laurasia Mattingly** is a meditation and mindfulness instructor and Reiki Master based in Los Angeles. After the loss of her mother, and experiencing debilitating anxiety, Laurasia spent years exploring her own spirituality, and found her passion lies in teaching people to live by the way of the heart. Laurasia guides her students by sharing the tools to find peace, joy, and, ultimately, happiness in the present moment.

She remains committed to her practice by pursuing additional education through the UCLA Mindful Awareness Research Center's MAPs courses, and attending silent retreats annually. Laurasia works with clients who are leaders in their industries and elite companies including Coachella Valley Music and Arts Festival, Soho House, Kaiser Permanente, Moët & Chandon, Nike, Lululemon Athletica, HUM Nutrition, Dogpound, and SB Projects, to name a few. She is the founder of her own virtual meditation platform, Sit Society, and leads retreats around the world. To learn more, visit LaurasiaMattingly.com.